I0212661

PENTATONICSOLOING
FORELECTRICBASS

Master & Use Pentatonic Scales as a Framework for Improvisation

JIMMYHASLIP

With Tim Pettingale

FUNDAMENTALCHANGES

Pentatonic Soloing for Electric Bass

Master & Use Pentatonic Scales as a Framework for Improvisation

ISBN: 978-1-78933-429-6

Published by **www.fundamental-changes.com**

Copyright © 2024 Jimmy Haslip

Edited by Tim Pettingale

The moral right of this author has been asserted.

All rights reserved. No part of this publication may be reproduced, stored in a retrieval system, or transmitted in any form or by any means, without the prior permission in writing from the publisher.

The publisher is not responsible for websites (or their content) that are not owned by the publisher.

www.fundamental-changes.com

Join our free Facebook Community of Cool Musicians

www.facebook.com/groups/fundamentalguitar

Instagram: **FundamentalChanges**

For over 350 Free Guitar Lessons with Videos Check Out

www.fundamental-changes.com

Cover Image Copyright: EXImages / Alamy Banque D'Images

Bass transcription & notation by Johnny Cox

https://johnnycoxmusic.com/

Contents

Introduction

Whenever someone picks up the bass to learn it, very soon they'll be playing pentatonic scales. Pentatonic scales are one of the simplest and most accessible building blocks of music, and the basis for countless popular songs and instrumental tunes.

Pentatonics are a very important tool to me as a musician. They form the foundation of what I do and make up the majority of my improvisational language. I view pentatonic scales as the *core* of my vocabulary, then build on their simple framework in order to create more sophisticated ideas.

In this book, we'll begin with the humble minor pentatonic scale that beginners always learn but explore how we can get the most out of it. We'll look at how I add strategic notes to pentatonic patterns to create new sounds, depending on the type of feel or mood I want to create, and see how that idea can lead to playing more creative lines – all rooted in the familiar, robust pentatonic framework that is so easy to play. This way of thinking is a great approach to refining and building on what you already know.

Along the way, we'll also look at a range of different soloing techniques – ideas such as controlling note length to alter the feel of phrases and push or pull against the beat; mixing note lengths within a melodic line to create complex rhythms; playing lines with odd-note groupings; applying articulation effects, dynamics and more.

By the end of this book, my aim is to have equipped you with the tools to become a confident soloist with a new level of mastery of pentatonic scales and beyond.

I hope you enjoy it!

Jimmy

Get the Audio

The audio files for this book are available to download for free from **www.fundamental-changes.com**. The link is in the top right-hand corner. Click "Download Audio" and choose your instrument. Select the title of this book from the menu, and complete the form to get your audio.

We recommend that you download the files directly to your computer (not to your tablet or phone) and extract them there before adding them to your media library. If you encounter any difficulty, we provide technical support within 24 hours via the contact form.

For over 350 free guitar lessons with videos check out:

www.fundamental-changes.com

Join our free Facebook Community of Cool Musicians

www.facebook.com/groups/fundamentalguitar

Tag us for a share on Instagram: **FundamentalChanges**

Chapter One – The Minor Pentatonic Scale

The minor pentatonic scale is one of the simplest yet most powerful tools at the bass player's disposal. But just because it's simple, and highly accessible to learn, that doesn't mean it's routine or boring. When explored thoroughly, it can provide us with endless possibilities for soloing on bass guitar.

In this chapter, we'll briefly cover minor pentatonic scale construction, then look at a series of exercises that will enable us to play the scale anywhere on the neck. Next, we'll move straight into applying the scale in the context of a solo.

In the free audio download, you'll hear me play a complete solo for this chapter. We're going to break down that solo into a series of shorter examples and look closely at the ideas being used. You'll learn how to create motifs with the scale and how to apply other phrasing techniques to get the most from it.

The Minor Pentatonic scale

"Pentatonic" is the name given to any scale that has five notes per octave. The minor pentatonic scale uses the root, b3, 4th, 5th and b7 degrees of the natural minor scale to make up its five notes.

In this chapter we'll play over a fusion track that has an E Minor tonal center and use the E Minor Pentatonic scale (E, G, A, B, D) to create melodic ideas.

First, let's look at how this scale lays out across the neck of a regular four-string bass and learn some useful patterns for playing it. We'll begin very simply with patterns you know, but quickly move into some sequenced patterns.

The example below shows the basic scale pattern in the open position, utilizing the open strings (bars 1-2). Alternatively, we can use the full range of first position on the bass to avoid using open strings, apart from the low E (bars 3-4). And, purely for effect, we could briefly move out of first position and include a slide on the low E string to play the scale as in bars 5-6.

Exercise 1

Exercise 2 shows the scale played from its root note on the A string, 7th fret. Since we begin on the A string, this pattern descends to include the available scale tones on the low E string, then returns to the A string root.

Exercise 2

To complete the picture, here is the scale played from its low E string root in the higher register.

Exercise 3

While it's useful to know these very simple positions, our real aim is to map the scale across the fretboard. The first step in doing so is to play the scale *vertically* using the range of the neck, rather than *horizontally*, remaining in position. Here is the E Minor Pentatonic scale played from its open string root, up to the A note on the G string, 14th fret. Already, this sounds more like a melodic line that just a scale pattern.

In order to quickly change fretting hand position for this exercise, you can use legato slides. In bar one, the third finger will play the note at the 5th fret, then slide up to the 7th fret. The same motion is repeated on the other strings. Practice playing this movement to get it sounding smooth, with no delay in sounding the legato notes.

Exercise 4

That is just one way of ascending the scale, but we have a number of options for *transition points* (the point on the fretboard where we need to change strings to continue ascending). Here's one alternative that uses a different transition point on the A and D strings.

Exercise 5

It often makes logical sense to use different transition points when descending, compared to ascending. This example takes one route to ascend and a different one to descend, based on the most logical fingering approach for each.

Exercise 6

To get comprehensive fretboard coverage, we can look at this scale another way. Once we're familiar with the scale pattern, we can launch from any note in the scale. This opens up four additional horizontal positions across the neck.

First, we can play the scale from its second degree (G, the b3 interval). It's worth noting that E Minor Pentatonic played from its second degree is identical to the G Major Pentatonic scale.

Exercise 7

Moving up the neck, next we play the scale from its third degree (A, the 4th).

Exercise 8

Next, we play the scale from its fourth degree (B, the 5th).

Exercise 9

And, finally, from its fifth degree (D, the ♭7).

Exercise 10

Spend some time practicing these patterns. First play the scale from its root note, using the range of the neck. Play it several times, each time changing the point at which you transition across strings. Second, practice launching the scale from each scale tone to cover the five horizontal positions.

Practice playing these patterns as much as possible until they become automatic to you, and you don't even have to think about them – the shapes are just second nature.

The next step is to practice playing vertically across the neck, launching from each of the five scale tones and using different transition points when ascending and descending. I won't demonstrate all of the pattern options to you, because there are many variations. But this is something you can work on during your practice sessions. However, here are a couple of examples to get you started.

This exercise launches from the b3, ascends the neck using one route, then uses a different transition point on the way down, ending on the low E root note.

Exercise 11

This time we launch from the 4th. This exercise uses the same transition points descending and ascending. To execute this line smoothly, play a first finger slide on the G string, from the 7th to 9th fret, then play the 12th to 9th fret movement with a pull-off.

Exercise 12

Sequencing the scale

I must stress that it's vital to know all these patterns inside out, so that you can navigate the fretboard using the scale, horizontally and vertically, and jump into it at any point. Armed with this approach to playing the scale, there are numerous ways of turning this information into melodic material.

We can now begin to break away from playing linear scale patterns and use those patterns to sequence the scale in different ways. At the same time, we can make things more interesting by applying different rhythms.

Here's an example that moves through the same scale positions as Exercise 6, and combines 1/4 note, straight 1/8th note and 1/8th note triplet rhythms.

Exercise 13

Here's a mind-bending pattern for you to try. It launches from the root note on the A string, 7th fret, then ascends in fours. Play four notes up the scale from the root note, then return to play four notes starting from the b3, etc.

Halfway through bar four, however, the sequence is changed and now we descend in groups of five notes. Playing odd note groupings over a 4/4 pulse is a good test of our ability to count while maintaining the groove. Practice this exercise on loop to a metronome until you're really on top of the timing. Start at around 80bpm and work your way up to playing it smoothly at circa 130bpm.

Exercise 14

Augmenting the scale

If we use the pentatonic scale as the framework for our playing, we can then begin to introduce other colors by augmenting the scale with carefully chosen additional notes. In the solo that follows, you'll see that every now and then I include an F# or a C note. The idea here is to utilize the two notes from the E Natural Minor parent scale that are omitted when forming the E Minor Pentatonic scale.

You may ask, *well why not just play the natural minor scale then?*

The answer is that it would take us away from the simplicity and playability of our robust pentatonic shapes. When I look at the fretboard, I visualize the pentatonic shapes and see the notes sitting around them as additional colors I can use at will. (We will dig much deeper into this idea in Chapter Five).

Notice in the solo examples that I use those two additional notes very sparingly, usually to serve a motif pattern that I've begun, or to help transition smoothly between positions on the neck.

We can view these notes from the E Natural Minor scale like *approach notes* in jazz. It's common in jazz vocabulary to approach strong chord or scale tones by playing notes a half step below or above them. This idea is called *targeting,* where we play a passing note first, in order to highlight a specific chord/scale tone we're aiming for.

So, the F# note from E Natural Minor acts like a half step *below* approach note that resolves to the G note of E Minor Pentatonic.

And the C note is like a half step *above* approach note that resolves to the B note of E Minor Pentatonic.

When played over an E minor chord, the F# note makes an Em9 sound (E, G, B, F#). If we play the C note over an E minor chord it makes an Emb6 sound (E, G, B, C), adding a melancholy twist to the straight pentatonic scale.

Here's a simple exercise that shows the F# note being used as an approach note in the pickup bar to target the G scale tone that falls on beat 1 of bar one.

Exercise 15

And here's an example of the C note being used as a pivot note to move smoothly between positions.

Exercise 16

Creating melodic phrases

We've really only scratched the surface of working with the pentatonic scale to form patterns and sequences that will eventually help us to master it, but we'll do more work on sequencing in a later chapter. For now, hopefully I've given you enough information to work on these skills on your own. Spend as much time as you can playing the scale horizontally and vertically, and working out scale sequences that you like the sound of, which could be useful as licks.

Now it's time to move on and begin to use the E Minor Pentatonic scale in the context of a solo. Here we're going to expand on some of the techniques we've briefly touched upon, and also begin use the creative tools of the soloist.

I suggest that you listen to the audio of the complete solo first. Then we're going to break it down into smaller chunks to learn it. Some complicated rhythmic lines will appear as we progress, so always be sure to slow down and isolate ideas to learn them thoroughly.

One of the most simple but effective tools we have when soloing is the *motif*. Motifs are short melodic phrases that make a musical statement. They are found extensively in the jazz vocabulary but also in other styles of music, particularly the blues and classical music.

Motifs are often the building blocks of a well-conceived solo. Once the musical statement is made, it can be repeated and elaborated on, or altered in different ways, and doing so will create a theme for your solo. Motifs can make the difference between a solo sounding like a story, or random and disconnected.

In this first example, you'll notice the additional notes from the E Natural Minor scale appear, but in fact they are played only to mirror the keyboard part on the backing track in this instance.

A motif is played in bar three, then repeated in bar four. Rhythmically, and in terms of the note choices, this phrase establishes a musical idea that we then revisit and restate in different ways.

Example 1a

A simple melodic idea can become much more effective depending on how we phrase it. Although it's useful to have an in-depth knowledge of scales and how to apply them, if I could advise you to work on just one area of your playing, it would be feel and timing.

Playing something simple that feels really good will always trump something complex, because an audience will always respond to great feel.

Have a close listen to the audio of this example. The opening phrase is played slightly behind the beat so that the D note at the 12th fret "floats" over the bar line into bar two. After this "slow note", the next note is placed before the beat, preceded by a grace note, so that it anticipates what's coming next.

It is this subtle pushing and pulling of the notes that creates a strong feel. Notice at the end of bar three that the motif is restated, but here it has been displaced (moved to a different beat in the bar) so that it crosses the bar line.

Example 1b

Example 1c is a short idea that states a new motif on the higher strings. Notice that the phrase is positioned to span two bars, starting on beat "2&" in bar one. In bar two, the phrase ends a fraction before beat 2, but then vibrato is applied to the note to allow it to sustain subtly and float over the beat.

Example 1c

Example 1d is a development of this idea, and we revisit it in bar three. However, rather than playing straight 1/8th and 1/16th notes as in the previous example, this time it has a subtle 1/8th and 1/16th note triplet feel. Superimposing triplets over a 4/4 groove is a great way to break up the rhythmic feel.

Example 1d

This phrase is a development of the previous motivic idea. Notice here that placing the start of the phrase on beat "4&" of bar one gives it a sense of urgency as it anticipates beat 1 of bar two.

Example 1e

We've touched upon the idea of augmenting the E Minor Pentatonic scale by adding F# and C notes from the E Natural Minor scale, especially if they can serve to form a melodic sequence. This next line is an example of that, as we play in a single position and limit ourselves to mostly using notes on the top two strings.

As an exercise for your practice times, imposing limitations on yourself can be a great way to stimulate creativity. For instance, try limiting yourself to just two strings and a four-fret range while jamming over a tune or backing track. Your goal is to generate as many melodic ideas as you can, while confining yourself to those notes. You'll notice that you soon turn to more rhythmically interesting ideas than you might otherwise have played, to get the most out of the notes.

Example 1f

In the next example, we open with a lick that echoes the theme of Example 1e. Creating this kind of continuity in your solos will help to glue your musical ideas together and turn them into stories, so they don't sound like random noodling. Repeating and making small alterations to motifs can make all the difference.

Example 1g

Listen to the audio and you'll hear that examples 1h and 1i are played over a drum breakdown on the backing track. This first line is all about the articulation of the phrase.

Another valuable asset in the bass player's armory is *dynamics*.

When playing bottom end basslines, consistency of volume and tone is very important, but to achieve a more vocal approach in our phrasing when soloing, dynamics are key. Here, we are hitting scale tones on the beat and making them pop out by playing them more loudly than the surrounding notes.

The articulation of these notes is important here too. The main emphasis notes are preceded with a legato slide but then played with a slightly more staccato feel. This adds to the listener's impression that we really want those notes to count!

Example 1h

The second part of this idea, played over the drum breakdown, is a busier line featuring a 1/16th note run in bar two. The line ends before the beat and vibrato is added so that the last note floats over the bar line.

Example 1i

The next phrase is played behind the beat to give it a laidback, bluesy feel. It's always tempting to fill space, especially when soloing, but leaving space between phrases makes the solo seem like it has more rather than less.

Example 1j

You may have noticed there are quite often dotted 1/8th and 1/16th notes in the notation. Controlling the length of notes, i.e., deciding when to cut them short or allow them to sustain, has a great impact on the feel of what we play.

As I'm sure you know, a dotted 1/8th note is held for the value of an 1/8th note and half as long again. Dotted 1/8ths and 1/16ths are especially useful for achieving a sense of floating over the groove when soloing – the opposite of locking into the groove when playing low bassline parts.

Example 1k

Another way of thinking about motifs is to make a *rhythmic motif* and vary the notes. That's the idea used in this example, where the rhythmic figure is similar, but the idea is moved to a higher string set. Using similar rhythms for phrases gives your audience a solid, melodic frame of reference to hang onto.

Example 1l

The next example begins with a phrase that pushes and pulls the timing of the line over the groove. The repeated B note at the beginning creates a sense of urgency and pushing forward, while the 1/4 note triplets at the end of the phrase really pull it back.

In itself, the shape of the phrase is not difficult to play, but it's the note length control that makes it stand out.

Notice that as bar three transitions into bar four, I used a C# chromatic passing note to target the D note that falls on beat 1 of bar four, then repeated this note before completing the phrase.

Example 1m

Example 1n is another example of working a limited area of the fretboard. Apart from a couple of notes, the majority of this line sits in a two-fret zone. The resulting line is necessarily composed as a strong, rhythmic figure, and in bar one we make use of some modern sounding 4th intervals.

Example 1n

This four-bar section of the tune precedes the set-piece ending of Example 1p. The phrase includes a long-held A note and plenty of space. Have a listen to the audio to capture the phrasing and articulation of the notes.

Example 1o

18

This final example is all about locking back in with the keyboards and playing with (and around) the specific accents the band are highlighting.

The full backing track without my bass is included in the audio download, so you'll be able to practice locking in with the groove on this example and, of course, I hope you have fun just jamming over the whole track!

Example 1p

In the next chapter, we're going to explore a new track with a different vibe in a different key, and work on expanding our range of melodic soloing ideas.

Chapter Two – Cool Vibes (Intermediate Solo Study)

Cool Vibes is a funky tune in the key of C Minor. In this chapter and the next, we'll look at a range of melodic ideas we can play over it. The ideas are simpler in this chapter, with more advanced phrasing in the next.

Soloing is all about building a vocabulary and, if you're prepared to put in the work, your vocabulary can become extensive. It works in exactly the same way as we might learn any language: we start by learning simple phrases as the basis, then we keep adding to them, until eventually we can begin to put together more advanced phrases.

Then we move on to learn the subtle nuances that native speakers of the language have – the types of expression that can't be found in standard language dictionaries or guides. And, if we keep going, eventually we can become fluent in the language. It's the same process with music, and it just takes time.

In order to become fluent, it's important to listen a lot. You can, of course, listen to other bass players, but you should also learn from other instruments.

I was privileged to hang out a lot with Jaco Pastorius over the course of a year and have lessons with him. As exceptionally gifted as he was on his instrument, he was a life-long learner and he never stopped practicing. One piece of advice he gave me was to listen to horn players, because the great horn players know how to solo and they have a single-note instrument. From that moment I started listening to a lot of horn players!

I once shared an apartment with Robben Ford in Hollywood, so I also listened to a lot of guitar players during that time. Whatever I listened to, I took something from each musician – and not just the notes, but the attitude with which they played. The feel was important, the sense of timing, and especially the phrasing.

Listening to how different players used dynamics was also an education. We can play loud notes or quiet notes, long or short notes, fast bursts or slow soulful notes. Just doing that, we already have six different ways of articulating our melodic ideas. Bear this in mind as we work through this piece.

Before we get into the main section of the tune, there is a head section. At the end of the first time around the head, the bass joins in with the keyboards to play the melody in Example 2a. All the notes come from the C Minor Pentatonic scale (C, Eb, F, G, Bb).

Example 2a

As the head is played for the second time, the bass doubles the melody with the keyboards again. We continue to draw the notes from the C Minor Pentatonic scale. When you've learned the bass part for the head, practice it to the provided backing track.

Example 2b

Following the head, we get into the main section of the tune. Here, the overall tonal center of the tune is C Minor, though you'll hear the guitar accompaniment on the backing track playing a range of C Minor-related voicings.

In bars 1-3, these chords are based on harmonizing the C Dorian scale in 4ths to produce a set of quartal voicings – an idea that occurs frequently in the playing of McCoy Tyner.

Normally, we take the notes of a scale and harmonize it in 3rds to produce its diatonic chords, but stacked 4ths produce a more modern sound and creates some interesting tensions.

The C Dorian scale contains the notes: C, D, Eb, F, G, A, Bb

Starting on the root note, if we stack every 4th note we get C, F, Bb, Eb, which spells a Cm11 chord.

If we repeat the process from the next note in the scale (D) we get D, G, C, F, which is Dm11.

And, starting from the Eb note, we have Eb, A, D, G, which spells Ebmaj7#11.

In bar four, we deviate from the quartal harmony with a Cm9 chord.

We're borrowing some C Dorian notes to play over these chords. In a later chapter, I'll show you exactly how I visualize Dorian scale notes sitting around a pentatonic framework, but for now, I just want you to trust your ears and absorb the sound this makes.

This is a spacious line that seeks to spell out the harmony using question and answer style phrasing. In bar one, the opening phrase begins on beat "4&". In bar three, we begin the phrase on beat "3&". Not beginning phrases on the beat is an easy device to use if you want to express a more laid-back feel.

Example 2c

The C Dorian scale is nearly identical to C Natural Minor, but has a natural 6th rather than a b6 (A instead of Ab). Over a C minor chord, this interval implies a Cm6 or Cm13 harmony.

In bar one, we start on beat 4 with a Dorian-inspired phrase. In bars 3-4, the phrase is straight C Minor Pentatonic.

The phrasing in bar three is a little tricky. The first five notes are 1/8th note triplets. If you imagine a six-note phrase (which would be easy to count in triplets), I've just left out the first note.

The five-note phrase that takes up the rest of the bar is played as 1/8th note quintuplets. This has the effect of slowing down the phrase, which floats over the groove. I recommend listening carefully to the audio to capture the feel and phrasing.

Example 2d

In this example, to pin down the phrasing, I suggest isolating bar two to practice first, due to its mixture of rhythms.

First, play the 1/8th note quintuplet phrase that spans beats 1 and 2. The straight 1/8th note phrase that follows begins exactly on beat 3, so your goal is to get those first five notes in bar two sounding of equal length, in time to drop on the four-note phrase on beat 3.

Again, moving from 1/8th note quintuplets to 1/8th notes has the effect of slowing down the phrase.

Example 2e

Here's a simpler melodic phrase formed with C Minor Pentatonic.

Example 2f

In the next section of the tune, the harmony opens out and includes more colorful voicings, but they can all be related back to the overall tonal center of C Minor in some form.

For example, the notes of Abmaj7 can also be interpreted as a C minor chord with a b6. And over a C bass note, an Abmaj7#11 chord makes a suspended Cb6 sound.

In this line, I went for a bluesy phrasing approach using C Minor Pentatonic. Note the 1/4 step bend, otherwise known as a "blues curl" in bar seven.

We need to make one alteration to the C Minor Pentatonic scale in bar four to accommodate the harmony, when we're playing over the Eb(Maj7)#11 chord. The chord has a Gb note, whereas the scale contains a G.

When playing this line, use deliberately "lazy" phrasing in order to play slightly behind the beat. It's all too easy to play fast and rush ahead of the beat. When you feel like you're playing the phrase almost *too* lazily, you've probably got it just right.

Record yourself playing over the backing track and listen back to judge your timing. It's amazing how revealing a recording can be!

Example 2g

Next, the previous eight-bar section of the tune is repeated. The chords are the same here, apart from a brief Bmaj7#11 passing chord that occurs at the end of bar eight. (Over this chord we play just one note – an Ab – which is its stable sounding 6th interval).

Scale-wise, in bars 1-4 the melodic ideas are based around C Dorian (although in this phrase we're not using the characterful natural 6th). In bars 5-8 we switch to the C Natural Minor scale, which is immediately identifiable by its b3 (Eb) and b6 (Ab) intervals.

When playing in the upper register of the bass, because there is naturally more clarity and separation between the notes, it's tempting to play something fast. We can, and will, do that in due course!

But this zone of the instrument also really lends itself to vocal phrasing, so it's important to work at playing phrases that have great articulation and "float" over the beat, just like a singer would. Try to inject as much emotion into these high-register phrases as you can.

Example 2h

Now we are back to playing over the head section of the tune to finish. This time around, rather than doubling what the keys are playing, we will take a counterpoint approach and play a line that complements the arrangement.

When playing pentatonic ideas, I'm always looking for ways to produce melodic phrases that are not just running up and down the scale, and this is where sequencing is a great approach. In other words, creating a pattern of notes in an order that is not wholly stepwise. In bars 5-6, you'll play a sequenced phrase that avoids the stepwise motion of the scale and organizes many (though not all) of the notes into 3rd intervals.

Example 2i

We've had one run through this tune and eased our way into it. In the next chapter we're going to up the complexity and play more advanced ideas.

Chapter Three – Cool Vibes (Advanced Solo Study)

In this chapter we're going to work through the same tune but explore more advanced phrasing ideas than in the previous chapter.

This time, we start by playing a highly syncopated line over the head section of the tune. All the notes come from the C Minor Pentatonic scale and the idea draws from the influence of horn players.

Saxophonists often use a technique called double-tonguing, whereby a note is repeated in rapid succession. Transferred onto bass, we can emulate this idea by repeating notes within a flowing, legato, saxophone-style run.

Using this idea is also a great way of breaking up the pentatonic pattern and avoiding just running up/down the scale. In this line you'll find repeated notes throughout, and this somewhat disguises the pentatonic nature of the pattern.

You'll also need to practice the syncopated rhythm to get this line down. It is mostly organized into 1/8th note triplets, but in bars 2-3 these are punctuated with four-note groupings of straight 1/16th notes. The effect is one of speeding up slightly, then slowing back down.

I suggest setting a metronome to around 60bpm to learn the timing of the phrase, then gradually increase the tempo until you're ready to try it over the backing track.

Example 3a

During the next part of the head, I wanted to capture a more vocal-like line in the high register, which would complement what the keyboards are playing. For this, I opted for the C Natural Minor scale, which adds the sounds of the b6 (Ab) and 9th (D) to our pentatonic framework.

The line is a motif-based idea with question-and-answer phrasing.

Example 3b

We continue with the C Natural Minor scale for the last section of the head. One of the best tools we have when creating phrases (and one that's not often discussed) is to use space in our lines by controlling note length. We can play the same lick, one time holding onto the notes for their full duration, and again playing certain notes staccato. Plus, we can break up melodic ideas by introducing rests.

Horn players are great to listen to because they are forced to take a breath between phrases. This results in a naturally more melodic approach, which makes their ideas easier to digest for their audience. Because we bass players don't have the same constraints, it's all too easy to forget to "breathe" when we phrase.

If we count bar one in 1/16th notes, "1-e-&-a, 2-e-&-a, 3-e-&-a, 4-e-&-a", then the first phrase begins on the "a" of beat 1, a fraction before beat 2 drops.

It's a six-note phrase, the first five of which are all 1/16th notes, before we play a staccato 1/8th note. After an 1/8th note rest, two more staccato 1/8th notes are played.

This sounds complicated in words, but listen to the audio and you'll get it.

The result of this phrasing idea is that it creates space and dynamics. If we played this line allowing all the notes to ring for their full value, the feel would be dramatically different. It wouldn't be "wrong" to play it that way, but I want to alert you to the dynamic control that is available in your fingertips.

As the line continues, you'll see that we continue to control note length to make the phrase groove, and we mix up the rhythms a little in the final two bars.

Example 3c

Now we get into the main body of the tune, and here is a line that features a complex rhythmic approach.

In bars 3-5, this is the kind of the line that is easier to understand when heard than to see it written down, so first check out the audio and listen to the example a few times.

In bar three, the phrase begins on beat 2, where we play an 1/8th note followed by two 1/16th notes.

The next part of the phrase, which is 1/8th notes played as a group of seven, begins right on beat 3.

The important thing here is to slow things down and practice playing seven notes of equal length spanning two beats, because it's easy here to go too slowly, then rush the last couple of notes.

In bar four, split this line into two halves: the seven-note phrase consisting of 1/8th notes, then the five-note grouping of 1/16th notes, followed by one 1/8th note.

Learn them separately, then combine them.

Example 3d

This next line is easier to play rhythmically, as it's mostly straight 1/16th notes, apart from the last three notes of bar two, where introducing 1/4 note triplets slows the line down a little.

We begin with a straight run up the C Minor Pentatonic scale, beginning on the b3.

In bar two, it's helpful to think of this pentatonic scale sequence as groups of four-note cells, which we then connect together. Each cell is a short melodic phrase in its own right. They are like individual words, which we then form into a sentence.

Example 3e

Next, try this descending C Minor Pentatonic sequenced line.

Again, we're mixing up the note groupings to keep the phrasing interesting and allow the line to float over the beat.

The line itself is made up of a repeating six-note motif. It is first stated at the beginning of bar two. Thereafter, it's always preceded by two lead-in notes. Take those lead-in notes away, and you'll hear the motif repeated in different registers.

If you can apply this kind of cellular thinking to your playing, then you'll be able to get more mileage out of every melodic idea you play and create some interesting long lines.

Example 3f

The useful thing about having a pentatonic framework on which we base our ideas, is that we're working with a very familiar structure that we can add to if we want to create a certain effect (rather than thinking of a whole new scale).

At the beginning of this line, we "borrow" the Ab note of the C Natural Minor scale to play over the Cm11 chord, which briefly implies the sound of a more colorful Cmb6 harmony. This is the only time that note occurs in this line, but we always have the choice to add notes around our pentatonic patterns to make a line more interesting.

Notice at the beginning of bar two and the end of bar four that I apply a fast vibrato to the Eb notes. Vibrato is an articulation technique that is quite personal to every player. A rapid vibrato has become a feature of my playing, but everyone does it differently.

Some player's vibrato is so distinctive (take Jeff Beck as an example) that they only have to play one note, and everyone recognizes who's playing. Experiment with your own vibrato to find a sound that fits your personality and voice.

I suggest working out the fingering and phrasing for bars 3-4 in isolation before attempting the whole line. Again, we have a phrase comprising seven 1/8th notes. This is followed by three lots of four-note cells. The seven-note phrase is a straight run up the C Minor Pentatonic scale starting from its 4th degree. It's an easy pattern, so focus on getting those seven notes sounding equal over beats 1 and 2.

Example 3g

In this next example, we add an additional D note to our pentatonic framework to give it another color. Borrowed from the C Natural Minor scale, when played over C minor, D is the 9th interval of the chord, but we use it mostly in bars 3-4 where it functions as the major 7th of the Ebmaj7#11 chord.

You may notice that we don't play the #11 (A) of this chord at any point. We certainly could, if we wanted to especially highlight that tension note, but as a soloing strategy I recommend that you focus on the stable chord tones most of the time, and don't rush to play the altered notes.

For example, if you see on a chord chart a ii – V written as Dm9 – G13b9, that's already a lot of information to think about.

However, for the Dm9 chord we can play the root, b3, 5th or b7, and for the G13b9 we can play the root, 3rd or b7. Using a combination of these notes, we haven't had to worry about any extended or altered notes, and we've still spelled out the sound of the harmony.

Take this approach the majority of the time and you'll have a strong foundation onto which you can then add other tensions.

Example 3h

Example 3i is all about the articulation. When you play this line, aim for a vocal-like phrasing and inject as much emotion into the notes as you can. Adding your personal vibrato will help here.

In bar two, the high F note that is emphasized is the 11th of the underlying C minor chord. A mixture of rhythms helps to keep this line interesting, and we are varying the dynamics: two slower vocal phrases are punctuated by a busier 1/8th note triplet phrase.

Example 3i

In the next part of the tune, the harmony changes to Abmaj7, followed by two major 7#11 chords. In bar four, we have the very tense sounding Bmaj7#11, which is a passing chord that wants to resolve back to the overall C minor tonality.

This is one occasion where we might choose *not* to stay safe, and decide to highlight some altered notes, because the chord is so different and doesn't belong to the parent key. In this short phrase, the Db note is the 9th of the chord, then we play the root note. After that, the C is the b9, then we play the #11 (Ab) and finally the #5 (G).

If those note choices seem a bit overwhelming, remember that when a chord like this appears on a chord chart, you can still work with just the root, 3rd and 5th until you've had time to think through adding some of those more colorful tones!

Example 3j

For the final two examples, we're back at the head of the tune. Once again, we play some melodic lines over this section, rather than trying to copy the keyboard part.

We start with a vocal phrase. Work on capturing the laid-back feel here and add your own style of vibrato to the high G note.

In bar three, we're coming back to an idea we've used before to break up the rhythmic pattern. Where we could have played a constant stream of 1/8th note triplets, after the first grouping of three we add in a group of four 1/16th notes, then return to 1/8th note triplets. This gives the effect of briefly speeding up the line, and makes it more unpredictable.

Make the most of the vocal phrase at the end of bar five.

Example 3k

The Ab note of the C Natural Minor scale is used frequently in this last example. The b6 tone implies a Cm6 harmony, which creates a pleasing tension.

The line is broken up rhythmically to add interest. Notice in bar two that we cut off the third note in both triplet figures, which adds some unexpected space into the phrasing.

Again, in bars 3-4 the rhythms are constantly changing to bring that sense of unpredictability.

Example 31

Chapter Four – Composition Challenge

It's essential to study theoretical musical concepts and learn how to apply them by playing isolated licks and lines that illustrate them; then practicing those ideas until we begin to absorb them into our vocabulary. However, most musicians will identify with the fact that there always exists a gap between what we'll play when sitting in the practice room, and what we're inclined to play when we find ourselves in a live or recording situation. Although we may have lots of ideas "in theory", often this thinking goes out of the window when the recording light comes on!

As a brief respite from technically developing our pentatonic framework, in this chapter I want us to take a look at what I'll call *real world* soloing. We'll study two solos I recorded for album tracks and analyze what was played. We'll also consider the context of each tune and how the vibe influenced what was played.

Then, using the backing tracks of the complete songs, I want to set you the challenge to compose your own solo for each track, using any and all of the ideas we have explored so far. This will be a great learning exercise for you to apply what you've learned on a blank canvas, led by your own creativity and ideas.

If you have an appropriate set-up to do it, it will be a great exercise for you to load the backing track into your DAW software, hit record, and do a one-take solo with little or no preparation, just to see what you come up with.

Listening back to a solo can be a very revealing (not to mention sobering) experience. Listening to ourselves immediately highlights areas of our playing that need to be fixed – such as timing issues or sloppy phrasing. It also makes the good ideas we had stand out from the rest.

Armed with this information we can say to ourselves, "OK, I need to do more of *this* and less of *that*! This process will also challenge you to think more melodically and put music first over technique.

Next, having improvised a solo, try composing one in a slow, considered manner, then practice it and record it.

Compare the two solos, take away the ideas you liked, and discard the ideas that didn't work. Then go back and record a third solo. Editing your playing like this will quickly help to refine your technique and distil your best musical ideas.

But first, let's look at what I played on these two tracks.

First, we'll look at the tune *Trinity One* from the album of the same name by my friend Ray Lyon. Then we'll look at a tune called *Lazaro*, which was featured on the Yellowjackets album *Lifecycle*.

Trinity One – Breakdown

The tune *Trinity One* is in the key of F Minor and throughout the solo Ray plays some very hip chord voicings on piano that give the piece a beautiful, ethereal feel, and provide the perfect canvas for a bass solo.

I rarely use effects, but the spacey vibe of this tune seemed to call for it, so I added some digital delay. A great biproduct of this decision was that it forced me to play phrases with clear "breaths" in between, so that the delayed notes didn't get muddied up.

The complete solo from start to finish is included in your audio download, as well as each individual example. Learn all the component parts first, then put them all together to play the full solo.

You'll notice in this solo that no phrase ever begins on the downbeat of bar one. This is because the structure of the solo is like a question and answer interplay between the piano and the bass. Most of the time, the piano will sound some chords and the bass will answer with a phrase.

In Example 4a, we're using the F Natural Minor scale as the source for our melodic line, which comprises the notes F, G, Ab, Bb, C, Db and Eb.

Although the overall harmony here is F Minor, at the beginning of the solo the chords take a more modal approach with a Dm11 and Gbmaj7 that don't belong to the key of F Minor. That said, the notes of F Natural Minor have an interesting effect over the shifting harmony.

The Eb note that is emphasized over the Dm11 chord is the b9, for example, and the C note superimposed over the Gbmaj7 in bar three implies a Gbmaj7#11.

Example 4a

In this example, the main phrase is played over an Abmaj7 chord, diatonic to the key of F Minor. Here, I chose to compose the melody using the F Minor Pentatonic scale (F, Ab, Bb, C, Eb).

Example 4b

There are some lovely half step movements in the chords of this tune that add subtle harmonic shifts. Here, over the Gbmaj7 chord, we're still using the F Minor Pentatonic scale to form the melody, even though the chord is not found in the key of F Minor.

The idea of playing a pentatonic scale a half step below the root of a major 7 chord is a well-proven substitution idea and a shortcut to immediately conjuring up some extended and altered notes over the chord. In bar one the Ab is the 9th of the chord (Gbmaj9), the Bb is a chord tone (3rd) and the C note is the #11 (Gbmaj7#11).

Example 4c

In the key of F Minor, chord iv is Bbm7. This chord is played in bar two, but in bar one the quality of the chord is changed to a suspended dominant. At the beginning of this phrase, we're using a chromatic descent on the top string to target the Bb root of the Bb7sus. The next three notes are all chord tones, but the C at the end of bar one suggests a Bbm11 sound, as it anticipates the Bm7 of bar two.

Example 4d

Next we have a very sparse phrase that leaves lots of space. In bars 1-2 we continue with the F Minor Pentatonic scale. The note choices create one extended note (C) and one altered note (Eb) over the Gm7 harmony – respectively the 11th and b13, making a Gm11b13 sound.

Over the Dm11 chord, the Eb note in bar two is the b9 and F is the 11th.

We use an Ab note over Gm7 is bar four to imply a Gm7b9, and a C note over Bb7sus to imply Bbm11 again.

Example 4e

We're playing right in the top range of a four-string bass for the next part of the solo. The Eb note of F Minor Pentatonic infers a b13 tension on the Gm7. In bars 3-4, the note choices of Bb, Ab and F are shared by both chords, so fit over both these voicings.

Example 4f

To end the solo, a line composed mostly of 1/8th notes, with some embellishments – like the grace note into the C in the middle of bar two, and the chromatic pull-off phrase in bar three that leads into a pedal tone idea on an F.

Example 4g

We've focused on the tensions made by different note choices over the rich harmony backing, but remember that the main aim is to create vocal phrases, full of expression.

Now that you've played through all the individual phrases, practice the full solo with the backing track.

Example 4h – Full Solo

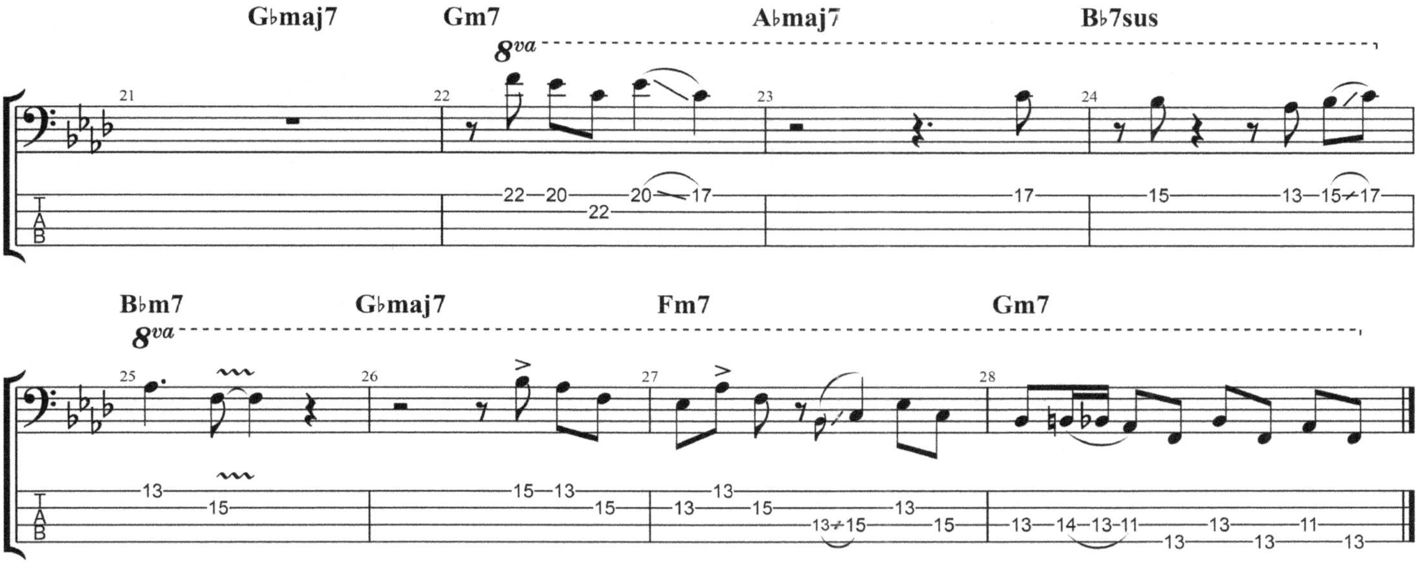
G♭maj7
Gm7
A♭maj7
B♭7sus
8va
B♭m7
G♭maj7
Fm7
Gm7
8va

Lazaro - Breakdown

In 2008, the Yellowjackets were recording their first album in 15 years to feature a guitar player. We collaborated with Mike Stern to produce the album *Lifecycle* and it proved to be a wonderful, creative time that resulted in a lot of high energy music. At that time, the core band consisted of Russell Ferrante on keys, Bob Mintzer on saxophones, Marcus Baylor on drums and me on bass.

Lazaro was one of two tunes I contributed to the album. I had begun writing it for a solo album I had planned, but in the end I felt it had more of a Jackets vibe to it, and would be fun to perform it with them.

The tune has a spacious, atmospheric feel and is played in 6/8 time. Marcus' careful placement of the snare drum accents on his groove creates more space, and then Russ's beautiful, minimalist chord voicings really open up the sonic landscape.

The early part of the track has a lot of momentum, so we decided to really bring things down for the solo, and I felt it called for a fretless bass. I wanted to inject as much feeling and emotion as I could into every phrase and leave plenty of breathing space between the ideas, not getting too busy with fast runs etc.

On the audio download, you have a recording of the entire solo, but also all the individual examples here, as we learn it phrase by phrase. You also have the backing track of the entire tune to play along to.

At the beginning of the solo, the harmony has an F7(add4) chord. This is an F7 triad with the b7 omitted and a Bb note added on top (the 4th or 11th), so the chord is spelled F, A, C, Bb.

The opening phrase is sparse, with slides and vibrato to create a vocal effect. The line begins on the 9th of the chord, sliding into the 3rd. Then we play the root and 11th. The high note in bar three targets the 5th (C).

These notes can be seen as coming from the parent scale of G Natural Minor, and in bars 4-6, I continue with a scalic line over Ebmaj7. Eb major is chord VI in the key of G Minor.

When playing this line, try not to rush, and instead play behind the beat, adding plenty of vibrato.

Example 4i

Now the harmony moves to an Ab triad inversion, with the 3rd as the lowest note (notated as Ab/C), which has the notes C, Ab, Eb.

With this phrase, we take the strategy of targeting the Ab root note of the chord right at the beginning. We use the G Natural Minor scale to form the phrase in bar two, then target the C chord tone at the end of bar three.

In bar four, the F note of the scale is emphasized and, over the triad inversion, implies the sound of Ab6.

Example 4j

Next we're playing over another inversion, this time of F7 (F, A, C, Eb), with the b7 in the bass. Over it, I play a Bb note in bars 1-2. This creates an F11 harmony – a similar effect to the F(add4) used earlier. In bars 3-4 we play a simple melody from the G Natural Minor scale.

Example 4k

In bars 1-3 of this section, we take a cellular approach to forming the melody, creating the phrase using just four notes from the G Natural Minor scale. In bars 4-6 the 5th of Ebmaj7 is highlighted (Bb) at the beginning and end of the line.

Example 4l

In this example, as we move to the Ab/C chord, we begin the line with an Abmaj9 arpeggio. I often like to play this arpeggio from its 7th (G) moving to the Ab root note, then ascending. Even though we are playing all chord tones, this half step movement sounds like a jazz-influenced chromatic approach note lick.

You'll notice that this line focuses on 1/8th note phrases rather than mixing up the rhythms. This idea is all about the articulation and the space between the melodic ideas.

Example 4m

In the next part of the tune the piano is playing an Abmaj7 chord. To create a moment of surprise here, we play a high D note and emphasize it. Over the Abmaj7 harmony, D is the #11, so it briefly adds a darker mood to the melody.

We're enriching the harmony of the Dm7 chord here too, repeating a G note through bars 4-6, which is the 11th of the chord.

Example 4n

To create a moment of tension over the Dm7 chord in Example 4n, in bars 1-2 we use the Bb note of the G Natural Minor scale. Over Dm7, the Bb introduces a b13 tension, which we pair with the stable 5th (A) of the chord.

In bar two, we include an Eb root note during the bar to signal the Ebmaj7.

Example 4o

To end the solo, here is a sequenced line. The notes come from G Natural Minor and the solo ends with the harmony moving to a Cm7 (chord iv in the key of G Minor).

To create the sequenced idea, I was looking for wider intervals and used several 5ths to construct the line.

Example 4p

Now that you've worked through every part of the *Lazaro* solo, try putting everything together and play along with the full solo.

Example 4q – Full Solo

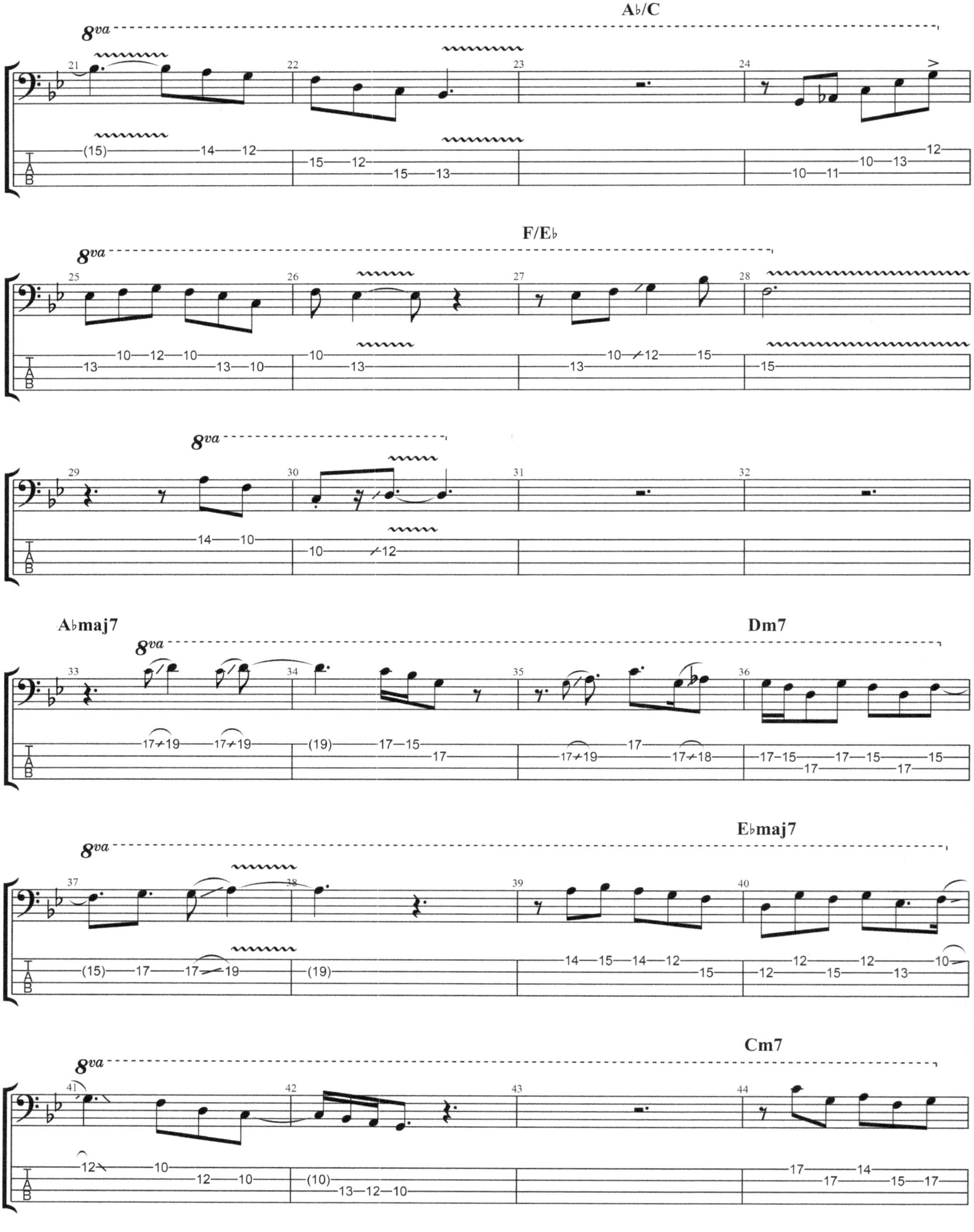
A♭/C
8va
F/E♭
8va
8va
A♭maj7
8va
Dm7
8va
E♭maj7
Cm7
8va

I hope you've found this insight into crafting a solo for recording a useful study. It's easy to blow over a solo, especially when playing live, because we don't usually have to account for the notes afterward! But when we know we're going to be listening to a solo we played for a long time to come, it's worth putting more thought and planning into what we play, and crafting something really melodic that fits the mood of the song.

Now, it's over to you. Improvise and then craft a solo over both tunes and, if possible, record yourself and then do some self-editing. Edit out those ideas that didn't work, and discover the ideas you'll want to keep and develop.

Chapter Five – Enhancing the Pentatonic Framework

In this chapter we return to the task of developing the pentatonic framework. Here, we are going to focus more intently on the skill of developing your bass soloing vocabulary, and we'll do so while practicing the art of soloing over a vamp.

In the genre of modern jazz-funk, it's very common for the head of a tune to be fairly complex in its harmony, while individual solos are improvised over one- or two-chord vamps.

On the surface, it sounds like it should be easier to play over just one or two chords, but this presents a different challenge to playing over complex changes. With the vamp, we can quickly run out of ideas, and the challenge is to keep things interesting. We can do so by mixing up our lines rhythmically, and also by introducing more colorful note choices.

When it comes to adding to the pool of available note choices for soloing, I always think in terms of enhancing the familiar pentatonic framework that we know so well, rather than thinking, "Now I'm playing a completely new scale." The advantage of this method is that we can keep all of the pentatonic language we know, and simply augment it with more colorful note choices.

Using pentatonic patterns as our foundation, it becomes easier to introduce passing notes or to "borrow" notes from other scales that will introduce extended notes or create more tension.

When necessary, it also becomes easier to *adapt* our pentatonic shapes to accommodate certain scale sounds we want to use, and we only have to think about moving one or two notes.

In this chapter we'll play to a drum groove provided by Nate Smith. Although there is no harmony underneath the bass parts, I had in mind playing over an Am7 – D7 vamp (chords ii and V in the key of G Major). The ii and V chords make a similar sound, so we can think of them as being interchangeable. In other words, the ideas we explore here will work if you're playing over just an Am7 chord, or just D7.

Before we get into other scale sounds, we'll start by looking at some more sequencing ideas using the A Minor Pentatonic scale. Because we're now playing in a new zone of the neck – and each zone presents new ways of visualizing the scale – let's start by drilling a few patterns to get warmed up.

In this first exercise, we play all five positions of the A Minor Pentatonic scale, arranged in an 1/8th note rhythmic pattern, ascending the neck. We repeat the first position an octave higher, so that we use the full range of the fretboard.

Start by playing this to a metronome set to 80bpm. Aim to play every note smoothly, controlling your dynamics, so that each note sounds at the same volume and for the same length. Keeping notching up the metronome in 10bpm increments, until you can play the exercise seamlessly with even dynamics at 120bpm.

Exercise 17

Now let's increase the difficulty of the exercise a little by ascending the first scale position and descending the next, then ascending the next, and so on.

Start with the metronome set to 80bpm and play through this steadily. Alternating between ascending and descending positions demands a strong visualization of the scale patterns on the fretboard. If you're struggling to visualize them, go back to the first exercise and practice each position for a while longer.

Once you're comfortable with the shape of this exercise, keep pushing up the tempo on your metronome. Aim for 140bpm this time!

Exercise 18

To make things a bit more difficult again, let's take Exercise 2 and play it as 1/4 note triplets. This means that the scale positions will no longer be neatly contained within the span of a bar. We'll have to think a little harder about transitioning between the shapes while keeping the pattern of triplets going.

Start this exercise with a metronome speed of 100bpm and work at getting it up to 140bpm.

Exercise 19

Now let's move the bar line again and speed things up by playing Exercise 3 in 1/8th note triplets, starting at 100 bpm.

To bring more definition to the triplet sound, emphasize the first note in each group of three. Keep pushing the tempo, but ensure you can play the exercise smoothly every time you notch it up.

Exercise 20

We're ramping up the difficulty again in Exercise 5. This time, we'll play the ascending/descending scale shapes in 1/8th note quintuplets. This exercise will help you to get to grips with this common odd note grouping.

Take the metronome back down to 80bpm, or slower, until you get used to counting ten notes over the four beats in each bar. Allow each note to ring for its full value and don't be tempted to rush and cram the notes in. It will take some practice to get the quintuplets sounding perfectly even.

Exercise 21

Next, we're going to combine two 1/8th note triplet phrases with a quintuplet phrase in each bar as we move through the ascending/descending scale shapes. 80bpm is a good starting point for this exercise. This version demands more concentration as we switch between the rhythmic figures.

Exercise 22

Next, we're going to break up the stepwise scale pattern by playing an ascending sequence arranged in diatonic 3rds. When we reach the top note of a shape, we'll descend the next shape in stepwise fashion.

It takes 12 notes to ascend each pentatonic shape and eight notes to descend it. This means that each ascending sequence will begin at different places in the bar and create a constantly shifting pattern.

Practice this starting with your metronome set to around 70bpm, or a little slower, until you've trained the pattern into muscle memory. Because we're using 1/16th notes this time, tempos of 80bpm and upwards will provide a challenge.

Exercise 23

Our last exercise is a "4s" drill. The idea is to begin on the root, ascend four scale notes, then return to the second note in the scale and ascend four notes from there, etc.

When you reach the top of a scale position, use a slide to move your hand into the next position. Then, you'll play "descending 4s". Continue this pattern up the fretboard.

I recommend starting this exercise with your metronome set to 65bpm. As you become more adept with the pattern, work towards a target of 90bpm.

We've warmed up by drilling the A Minor Pentatonic scale across the neck, now it's time to begin working on developing a vocabulary of vamp-based ideas. The first few examples here will focus on sequencing the A Minor Pentatonic scale, then we'll move onto exploring other scale sounds.

Developing Sequenced Pentatonic Scale Ideas

This first example is a saxophone-influenced line using the "double tonguing" idea of repeated notes that you might hear in a modern jazz sax solo. Since our pentatonic scale only has five notes, repeating some notes can help to fill out passages of 1/16th notes, as in bar two.

Think about the phrasing of this line. First of all, notice the placement of the rests.

We begin the phrase on beat 2 of bar one, then take a dotted 1/8th note rest. The remaining three notes in bar one are 1/16th notes, with 1/16th note rests between the first two.

This has the effect of punching out the notes to create a grooving syncopation. The last note of the bar is played on the "a" of beat 4 (i.e. "4-e-&-**a**") and held over into the next bar. This is another simple device that adds to the syncopation in the phrasing.

Bar two has a simple descending pentatonic sequence and we break up the phrasing by introducing a rest midway through the bar. Another rest at the beginning of bar three further breaks up the phrasing.

Example 5a

This line begins with an ascending scale run beginning on the b3. The next four notes also ascend the scale from the 5th. After that, we are just using the notes A, E and G in different permutations to create the sequence until we add another C note at the end of the bar. We end with a melodic triplet phrase in bar two.

This line is played quickly on the audio, so play it through several times and program it into muscle memory before bringing it up to tempo.

Example 5b

Next, here is a rhythmically complex sequence for you to try.

You've encountered the concept of combining quintuplet and triplet figures. This is more challenging because now you have to do it with 1/16th notes. As always, slow this line right down to learn both the shape of the line and the rhythmic placement of the notes.

Here is how I suggest approaching it:

Work on bar one in isolation to begin with. In bar one, we begin the phrase on beat "2&", and two 1/16th notes precede the quintuplet phrase. You need to fit those seven notes in before playing the first triplet phrase exactly on beat 4. Practice the timing of the phrase to a metronome set to modest tempo.

The two triplet figures at the end of bar one are part of a longer triplet phrase, so next work on combining all four groups of triplets, spanning the end of bar one into bar two. The phrasing will make sense to you when you put them both together.

Next, in bar two comes an eight-note phrase that mixes 1/16th and 1/32nd notes. Practice this phrase on its own to pin down the timing. It should have a kind of "bouncing" feel.

Now combine the two triplet figures at the beginning of bar two with the eight-note phrase.

When you've got that, the final phrase can be tagged onto the end.

Now go back and practice playing the whole line from start to finish.

Example 5c

In the next example, we begin on beat "3&" of bar one, and beat "1&" of bar two. It's always tempting to start phrases on the downbeat, especially in bar one, but by avoiding the downbeat we immediately create syncopation. What could be a routine kind of phrase will instantly sound much more interesting.

Bar two uses a melodic motif that repeats its phrasing.

If we are thinking in terms of playing over A minor, then in bar two, the first four notes (G, E, C, A) spell an Am7 arpeggio. The second group of four notes (D, C, A, G, beginning on beat 3) spell an inversion of Am11.

If we're treating this as a D dominant 7 vamp, then both sets of notes imply the sound of a D11 harmony.

Example 5d

When using the pentatonic scale it's easy to find ourselves just repeating phrases across octaves. Sometimes we want to do this, if we are stating then restating a motif. But often we'll want to bring variety into our phrasing and that means sequencing the scale differently, whether that's the patterns we choose to play or our note selection.

We begin this line with a simple pentatonic melody. Then, in bar two, we begin to sequence the scale as we descend.

A well-documented approach taken by saxophonists like John Coltrane and Michael Brecker is to organize scales into four-note cells in order to spell out chord sounds. The four-note cells don't have to contain four unique notes, one note can be repeated in order to spell out a triad sound.

Visually, you can see in the notation that bars 2-3 are organized using this approach.

A lot of different permutations can be derived from four notes! Most of these four-note cells spell out different inversions of an Am11 chord, with a couple of exceptions (C6 and Em7 cells are also present). The chords all belong to the parent key of G Major.

Example 5e

Here is another rhythmically complex run that combines 1/16th note triplets and quintuplets. Once again, the phrase begins on the "&" of beat 2.

In both bars, learn the phrases by first playing only the triplet groups to a metronome and count along in 1/4 notes, "1, 2, 3, 4".

Listen to how much space there is left in the bar. When you've assessed how much space there is for the quintuplet phrase to occupy, add it onto the triplet phrase and practice the complete line.

Whenever you're faced with some music that contains complex rhythms, always begin by breaking things down into smaller units. This is the best way to work out what's going on, and to understand how much space in the bar the note groupings occupy.

Example 5f

Next, play this descending A Minor Pentatonic sequence that uses four-note cellular units. The very first note of the first group of four is omitted.

This time, after two lead-in notes are played, sections of the scale sequence are organized into diatonic 4ths, i.e., A descending to E, G descending to D, then later, D to A and C to G.

Example 5g

This mixed-rhythm line makes more use of quintuplets in the second bar.

Starting with a fast trill in bar one, the idea here is to create a cascading downward lick. Rather than running straight down the scale, you'll notice that we keep jumping back a string as part of the sequence, which introduces some ebb and flow into the line.

In bar two, this is a good example of where repeating a motif down an octave can be very effective. But the phrasing is difficult, as we're using an eight-note phrase that begins with two triplets then takes the first two notes of the quintuplet.

This means that when the motif repeats, it begins part way through the first quintuplet and includes the whole of the next one.

Remember to break the line down into smaller units to learn the timing. When you get this line up to tempo it should sound as if it's cutting against the pulse of the drum groove.

Example 5h

Here is a variation on the previous line, this time beginning on beat 1 of the bar. Moving a lick to different beats of the bar is a very easy way to create variety in your soloing repertoire. The same phrase can sound completely different when placed somewhere else in the bar.

Example 5i

Adding Notes to the Pentatonic Framework

The beauty of the vamp is that its open sound gives us plenty of scope to introduce new tonalities into our vocabulary. We can experiment by adding different tensions then resolving them, and the addition of just one or two notes to our tried and tested pentatonic patterns can make a big difference to our musical language and the types of phrases we're able to produce.

Let me demonstrate this idea simply, before we move on to explore the two main sounds I like to use in my playing. The common blues scale is just the minor pentatonic scale with one added note:

A Minor Pentatonic: A, C, D, E, G.

A Blues Scale: A, C, D, **Eb**, E, G.

The blues scale introduces the "blue note" into our vocabulary, also known as the b5 interval, in this case an Eb. In the context of the minor pentatonic scale, the b5 interval instantly adds a bluesy feel to any line we play by creating a tension that is resolved to the stable sound natural 5th (E), or the 4th (D).

Here's an example line that includes the blue note, where the interplay is between the 4th and b5 intervals. This is a very common bluesy phrase, often played by guitarists.

All the blues scale does is to add *one note* to our pentatonic framework. This means that every pattern or sequence you already know can be adapted to include this new note.

Example 5j

Here's another example where we begin in A Minor Pentatonic in bars 1-2, then add the Eb note from the blues scale in bars 3-4. It is used more subtly here, but you can hear the blue note in the quintuplet phrase.

Example 5k

This is the concept in essence. Now let's move on to explore my two favorite ways of enhancing the standard pentatonic framework.

The Natural 6th of the Dorian Scale

Have a listen to the line in Example 51.

Which note stands out the most to you?

It's got to be the F# that falls on the "&" of beat 2.

In this line (which will work equally well over Am7 or D7) we're borrowing the F# note from the A Dorian scale (A, B, C, D, E, F#, G).

We can either add this as an "extra" note into the pentatonic scale, like we did with the blues scale, or we can adapt our pentatonic pattern and replace an existing note with the F#.

The latter is exactly the approach taken by the great jazz-fusion guitarist John Scofield and others. The idea is to take the minor pentatonic scale and *replace* its b7 interval with a major 6th, so that A, C, D, E, G becomes A, C, D, E, F#.

This hybrid scale is known as the A Minor 6 Pentatonic, and when played over an A minor chord it makes an Am6 or Am13 sound. When played over a D7, the F# note is a chord tone (the 3rd).

The diagram below shows the A Minor Pentatonic scale and the adapted shape to create the A Minor 6 Pentatonic.

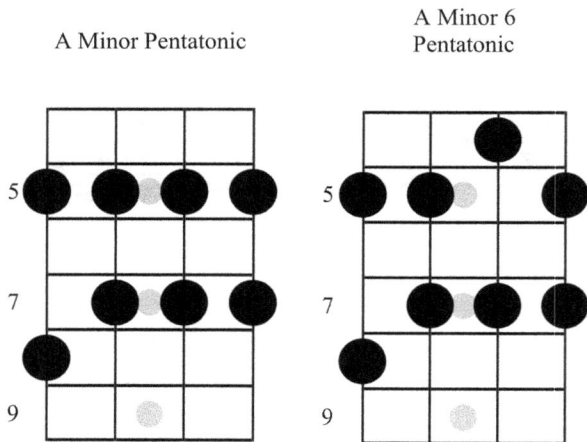

A Minor Pentatonic

A Minor 6 Pentatonic

I like to use this approach from time to time, but mostly I take the approach that we are using this extra note to augment and enhance our pentatonic patterns. Let's explore some vocabulary using this idea.

The first part of this line makes a feature of the F# note in the middle of bar two. This phrase also uses an *enclosure,* where we have a target note that we're aiming for and "enclose" it by playing notes above and below it.

Here, we play a scale tone above the target F# and a chromatic approach note below it. The use of the enclosure makes the F# stand out more.

The five-note phrase that ends the line reverts back to the straight A Minor Pentatonic scale.

Example 5l

This time the borrowed F# note is added by bending an F note up a half step at the end of bar two and allowing it to sustain.

Bar two uses the repeating rhythmic pattern of two groups of 1/16th note triplets followed by two straight 1/16th notes to break up the phrasing.

Example 5m

Here is a simple and very direct use of the Dorian note to enhance a pentatonic phrase. Whereas the minor 6 pentatonic scale replaces the b7 of the minor pentatonic, here we use both notes (G and F#) in an interplay to create a melody.

Example 5n

Next, a straightforward descending A Dorian lick. Harmonics are played in bar two, which over the A minor harmony outline an Am11 chord.

Example 5o

Here is another descending phrase that emphasizes the Dorian note on the G string throughout. Add plenty of expressive vibrato on the end of this phrase.

Example 5p

The Dorian F# is used throughout this rhythmically complex scale sequence. We're combining groups of 1/16th note triplets with 1/16th note quintuplets to vary the pace of the phrasing, again adding some fast vibrato at the end.

Example 5q

Bars 1-2 of this idea feature a chordal idea for contrast. After playing the b3 and 5th of the Am7 chord in bar one, the chord used in bar two implies an Fmaj7, which can be used as a substitution for Am7. (Am7 is chord iii in the key of F Major).

The rest of the line is an A Dorian scale sequence, but we don't play the F# character note in this instance. You can play the first three notes in bar three as a hammer-on/pull-off, or pluck every note if you prefer.

Example 5r

The Dorian Bebop Scale

In this next section, we're going to take the concept of borrowing from the Dorian scale a step further to augment our pentatonic vocabulary. This time, we'll extract an additional note to use from the *Dorian Bebop* scale.

Bebop scales are eight-note scales. The idea is to take a regular seven-note scale as a starting point, then add one extra note. This additional note functions just like a chromatic passing note, and is used to resolve to the next or previous note in the scale.

This is a core concept of jazz improvisation. The point of the technique is to create an eight-note scale that lends itself to playing long lines consisting of 1/8th notes. Long, flowing passages of 1/8th notes is a common feature of modern jazz, so it's incredibly convenient to have scales that contain eight notes instead of seven!

The notes of the A Dorian scale are:

A, B, C, D, E, F#, G

The Dorian Bebop scale adds a chromatic C#, so that we end up with:

A, B, C, C#, D, E, F#, G

However, what we're after here is an enhanced pentatonic shape that includes both of these character notes. The diagram below shows the "bebop" notes superimposed onto the standard pentatonic shape. As well as the two character notes (F#, C#) which distinguish the Dorian Bebop scale from the Natural Minor scale, I will often use the B note from the scale.

The addition of these notes, which fit neatly around the pentatonic shape, opens up many melodic possibilities.

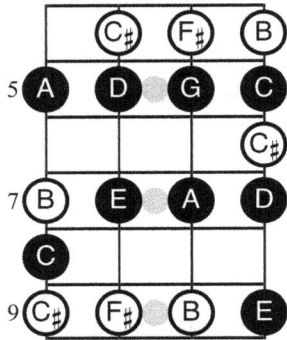

Let's see what we can do with this idea.

This first example uses just the C# note of the A Dorian Bebop scale and makes a feature of it at the end of the line by hammering onto it from the C scale tone. It definitely has a dissonant quality, and when played over an A minor represents a #9 tonality which adds an outside sound to any line.

Example 5s

Here is a more complex line that uses both borrowed notes of A Dorian Bebop. First of all, we feature the F#, hammering onto it in the opening phrase, and also landing on it on beat 1 of bar two. As with the regular Dorian scale, played over an Am7 vamp it represents the 6th or 13th interval, and over a D7 vamp it's a chord tone (the 3rd). The dissonant C# is saved for the end of the line in bar three, where we slide into it.

The B note, borrowed from A Dorian Bebop, just fell naturally into the shape of the line I played. This is the 13th of D7, and the 9th of Am7.

Example 5t

Here is a question and answer style phrase adding Dorian Bebop notes to the minor pentatonic framework. The C# note is emphasized in the opening phrase, at the beginning and end. The phrasing of this idea is copied in bar two, where only the borrowed B note is used.

Example 5u

This final example begins with a 1/16th note phrase before we alter the rhythm to play groups of 1/16th note quintuplets. The opening phrase is just A Minor Pentatonic, then B and C# notes are introduced into the quintuplet phrase.

Example 5v

The Diminished Scale

If I want to play the kind of lines that characterize the more "outside" aspect of jazz-fusion in order to create some tension and release, or just a little dissonance, I'll often use what I call the Double Diminished scale. Let's take a moment to understand what this scale is, before looking at how I use it when improvising.

The Diminished scale is an octatonic scale i.e., constructed from eight notes rather than the seven notes we'd expect when working with the major and minor scales and their modes. It's also a symmetrical scale, which means it follows a repeating pattern of interval steps.

There are two ways to play this scale: as a series of repeating "half step–whole step" movements, or a series of "whole step–half step" movements.

Named after the pattern of intervals they follow, the two modes of the Diminished are known as the Half-Whole Diminished scale and the Whole-Half Diminished scale, and use the following formula:

Half-Whole: Root H W H W H W H

Whole-Half: Root W H W H W H W

The A Half-Whole Diminished scale comprises the notes:

A, Bb, C, Db, D#, E, F#, G

The A Whole-Half Diminished scale has the notes:

A, B, C, D, Eb, E#, F#, G#

The Whole-Half scale is typically used to play over diminished chords, whereas the Half-Whole version of the scale is more suited to working over dominant 7 chords (or ii – V sequences).

Let's take a moment to talk about how I visualize this scale on the fretboard. If we fused together the notes of the A Half-Whole and A Whole-Half Diminished scales, we'd have every note of the chromatic scale and a complete "pool" of tension notes to draw from. But my starting point is still the minor pentatonic scale.

If we superimpose the notes of the A Half-Whole Diminished scale over the familiar A Minor Pentatonic pattern, we can visualize the tension notes sitting around the pentatonic scale shape.

A Minor Pentatonic
Scale

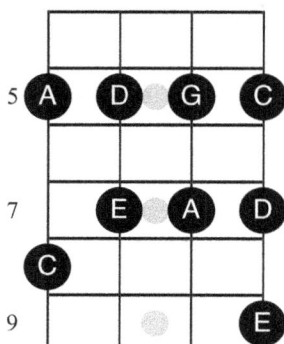

A Half-Whole
Diminished Scale

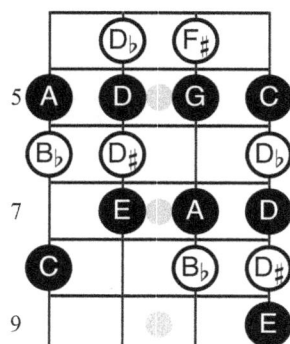

We can do the same with A Whole-Half Diminished.

A Minor Pentatonic
Scale

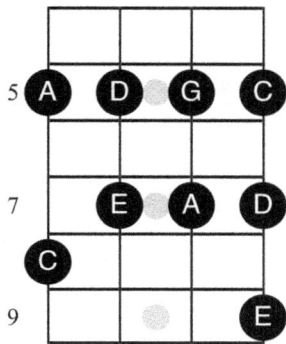

A Whole-Half
Diminished Scale

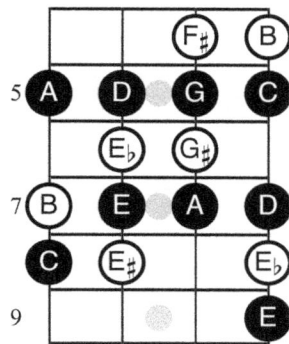

When I'm soloing, I'll keep the strong, pentatonic framework in mind, and I'll view all the tension notes that sit around it as places I can go to if I want to create a particular sound, either using the Half-Whole or Whole-Half pattern – and each tension note will have a different effect on the harmony.

Remembering that our vamp cycles between Am7 and D9 chords, here are a few examples of the tensions created using the notes of the A Half-Whole Diminished scale.

- Over Am7, the Bb note is the b9 and implies a spacious Am7b9 harmony. Over the D9 chord, it gives an altered sound, functioning as the #5

- Over Am7, the D# note (enharmonically Eb) makes an Am7b5 sound, and over the D9, it's the b9 for a D7b9 sound

- Over the D9, the F# note is a chord tone (3rd), and it turns the Am7 sound into an implied Am6, or Am13

Using the A Whole-Half Diminished scale shape, we have these additional tensions open to us:

- Over Am7, the B note creates an Am9 sound, and over D9 implies D13

- Over Am7, the F (E#) note creates a tense sounding Am7b13, while creating an altered dominant sound over D9 (D7#9)

- Over Am7, the G# note creates the unresolved sound of an Am(Maj7) chord, and turns the D9 chord into a D7#11

Overall, this approach is all about fusing together the solid, dependable tones of the minor pentatonic scale with these more exotic "destinations". We must rely on our ears to tell us which of these musical destinations appeal to us the most, and which ones we want to become an integral part of our vocabulary.

Now let's try some musical phrases using these diminished ideas.

This first example leads off with an F# tension note and also makes a feature of the Half-Whole's Db (C#) in bar one. In bar two, the line leads from the D# and includes lots of tension notes throughout.

To better understand how I arrived at such a line, let's take it back to the pentatonic framework for a moment, and visualize the fact that we are playing around these two shapes of the A Minor Pentatonic scale in the upper register. All the tension notes are within easy reach of one or other shape.

A Minor Pentatonic
Scale Shape 4

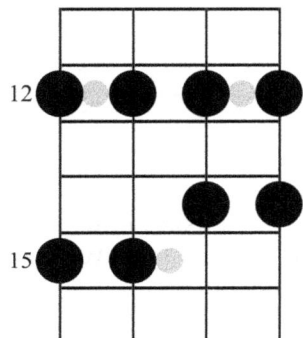

A Minor Pentatonic
Scale Shape 5

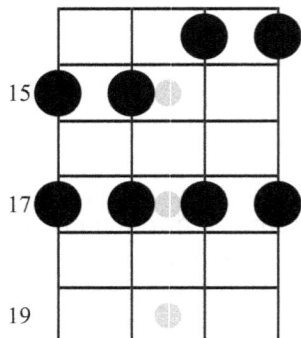

Example 5w

8va

```
—11—9—11—9—8———9——              —11-13-15-16-15-13——15-13———————11——  —9—9—
          —11————11—  —13-14—                    —16————16-13—11——11—
                                                                        —8—
```

Here's a diminished line that functions like a question and answer phrase. The first idea is stated lower down, then the answer phrase is played higher up.

In bar one, the line begins with notes from the Whole-Half scale, then we draw from both scales. In bar two the prominent tension notes are the C# and D#, which create dissonance over the Am7 – D9 harmony.

Example 5x

This line opens with a melodic phrase that relies on the G# note of the Whole-Half side of the diminished scale, which conjures up the sound of Am(Maj7) in bars 1-2.

At the end of bar two, we land on the D# again and add some fast vibrato. Now functioning over the D9 chord, this note is the #11.

Example 5y

The more experienced you get at using this technique, the more you'll become selective about your note choices. Here is a line that uses mostly the A Minor Pentatonic scale, but we borrow just the D# note from the A Half-Whole Diminished scale.

Looked at another way, we could say that we're using the A Blues scale here, with its added Eb. How we interpret a line will often come down to what we were visualizing and thinking about when we played it. Theory is just a way of describing a musical effect; the *sound* of what we play must always trump the analysis of the idea.

73

Example 5z

Next is a line that weaves between the two diminished modes. We begin with three notes from A Whole-Half Diminished, then follow with three notes from A Half-Whole. Then it's three more from the Whole-Half, then the Half-Whole again!

With persistent practice, you'll get better at viewing the two diminished modes as a seamless whole, which you can flow between.

Example 5z1

Here is one more line that fuses together the two diminished modes to form a complex outside-inside phrase. Notice the phrasing in this line, where we switch between 1/16th note triplets and quintuplets.

In bar two, the first five-note phrase revolves around the A Minor Pentatonic root note, and adds the F# and B of the Whole-Half to form a melodic cell.

The second five-note phrase uses the root and 5th intervals of the minor pentatonic and adds only the F#.

The third five-note phrase uses the pentatonic scale's 4th and 5th intervals, and adds F# and C# tension notes from the Half-Whole.

I highlight these structures to remind us that we can form endless melodic cellular idea using just a few notes, in the same way that John Coltrane did. Experiment with this idea and see if you can invent some of your own.

Example 5z2

Chapter Six – Advanced Minor Pentatonic Phrasing – Bringing it All Together

In this final chapter we are going to revisit the funky tune in E Minor that we began with in Chapter One. This time, we're going to ramp up the difficulty with more complex phrasing, and we're going to add more color notes, borrowed from some of the other scales we've looked at.

As we work through the solo breakdown, our aim will still be to control the note lengths and use different note length combinations to get a good feel, but this time the improvised lines will be much busier.

These examples include more odd-note groupings, which can be quite challenging to nail. When confronted with these, my advice is to isolate the difficult parts and slow things right down. Training your muscle memory and working on your time at a more modest tempo should put you on the right path.

In this first example, we're mirroring the keyboard part in bar one again, but with different note choices to the ones we used back in Example 1a. The idea is to imitate the part rhythmically, rather than play the exact same notes.

At the end of bar three, a G# chromatic passing note is used to target the 4th (A) of the E Minor Pentatonic scale. Throughout these examples, we'll occasionally borrow the C and F# notes that belong to the E Natural Minor scale, and a couple of other scales too. I'll point out where this happens.

Here, the C note from E Natural Minor is used to create the 1/16th note run up to a high D.

Example 6a

Example 2b features a descending sequence pattern that I often like to use.

You could think of this as a descending fours pattern in bar one, but the lick begins after a 1/4 note rest and includes a longer held 1/8th note before the 1/16th note descent.

This makes the phrasing trickier to pin down, and we also deviate from the initial pattern in bar two. Listen to the audio a few times then try playing along with me.

Example 6b

Here is an E Minor Pentatonic lick, augmented with just the C note from E Natural Minor. Make sure to play the first few notes of this line staccato, to make them pop out.

In bars 3-4 we have a mostly 1/16th note bluesy pentatonic phrase. We count 1/16th notes in a bar by saying,

"1-e-&-a, 2-e-&-a, 3-e-&-a, 4-e-&-a."

The phrase in bar three begins on the "a" of beat 2-e-&-a.

This can be difficult to count and pinpoint accurately. It will help you to focus on the C note at the 17th fret, which falls directly on beat 3. Think about playing that note dead on beat 3, but quickly precede it with the A note.

Example 6c

Example 2d is a challenging lick that features a descending run organized into quintuplets – an idea that I like to use a lot, both for its challenge and its musical unpredictability.

A quintuplet means that we fit five notes into the space where we'd normally fit four. In one bar of 4/4, we can play sixteen 1/16th notes, but we can fit in *twenty* quintuplets.

One of the challenges of playing quintuplets is to play all the notes evenly, keeping them to the same length. It's a big temptation to rush ahead because we naturally think, "I need to fit in four extra notes!"

If you feel you need to do a bit more work on this, I recommend the following practice exercise, played in 1/8th note quintuplets.

With the metronome set to 1/4 notes, you'll hear that it clicks on the *first* note in every group of five and the *middle* note of each group.

I suggest focusing on beat 1 to begin with. Aim to play evenly and hit the first note of each five-note group right on the beat. Record yourself if you're able. Once you're hitting the 1 comfortably, see whether you're also landing the middle note on the beat and adjust if necessary.

Bars 3-4 have 1/16th note quintuplets.

With your metronome set to 1/4 notes, it will click only on the first note of each five-note group, but you'll be playing the notes more quickly. I deliberately left out the final five-note phrase in each bar, replacing it with a 1/4 note rest, so you should complete this line then hear one click of the metronome at the end of each bar.

Repeat this exercise and slowly crank up the metronome a few beats at a time as you become more confident.

Exercise 25

Now onto the lick! It's played quite fast on the audio example, so I suggest slowing things right down to begin with and working out a comfortable and efficient way to finger it.

Once you've memorized the scale sequence, you can work on increasing the tempo.

Example 6d

Here is another quintuplet idea. In the previous example, the quintuplets were neatly contained in bar two, but this time we need to launch the scale sequence part way through a bar.

If we count bar one in 1/16th notes, the lick starts on the "&" of beat 3-e-&-a.

As before, practice the scale sequence first to commit it to muscle memory, then listen to the audio track a few times to get the timing in your head.

Example 6e

The next example is an E Minor Pentatonic line that is augmented by borrowing the C note from E Natural Minor in order to fill out the sequence.

In this idea, the first half of the line (bar one and the first three beats of bar two), is played tightly with the groove. The second half should be played with a looser feel that floats over the groove rather than strictly locking in with it.

This is difficult to convey in notation/TAB, so listen carefully to the audio example to get the feel right.

Example 6f

Now it's time for another E Minor Pentatonic quintuplet line in bar two of Example 2g. The five-note groupings are contained within the bar but pay attention to the end of the phrase where we break out of the pattern. The overall intention here is a fast but unpredictable bluesy lick!

Example 6g

Example 2h is perhaps the most rhythmically challenging line in the solo. It happens over the drum breakdown, so could be considered a "free time" idea because we don't have to worry about what the keyboard or guitar parts are doing at this point.

I wanted to play a kind of "outside-inside" line at this point, as the bass is unaccompanied. To that end, as well as using the E Minor Pentatonic scale, I drew melodic ideas from the E Whole-Half Diminished scale, which we explored in the previous chapter.

The Whole-Half scale comprises the notes E, F#, G, A, Bb, C, C#, D#. It shares E, G and A notes with E Minor Pentatonic, but its unique notes add a range of tensions.

As we're playing over an E Minor tonal center, those tensions include extended colors such as the 9th, 11th and 13th, and altered tensions including the #5 and #11.

The idea begins with the E Whole-Half Diminished scale, transitions briefly into E Minor Pentatonic in bar three, back to the diminished in bar four, then back to the pentatonic at the end of bar five.

Have a careful listen to the audio a few times, then slow things down and work with a metronome to capture the timing of the phrases. The mixture of note values means that some parts of it sound urgent, while other parts are more laid back.

Example 6h

After that difficult line, here's a simpler idea that uses only the E Minor Pentatonic scale and floats over the groove.

Example 6i

This next example borrows both F# and C notes to form the melodic ideas, plus a single passing F note.

After the 1/16th note run in bar two, pay attention to the phrasing and note values in bar three, where the 1/8th note triplets pull back against the groove, and the short staccato 1/8th notes break up the rhythm.

Bars 4-5 contain a rhythmic motif where the phrasing is similar, but the notes are different. The phrase is displaced, however, so that the second time it begins on a different beat in the bar.

Example 6j

Example 2k is another challenging, rhythmically complex line. Overall, the musical intention here is to play some bluesy licks, so in this line we borrow the Bb "blue note" from the E Blues scale.

The opening phrase begins on beat 2 of bar one. The note combinations are complex but essentially the phrase contains a fast trill at the beginning – similar to a hammer-on/pull-off – moving back and forth with the F# note on the D string, 16th fret. This acts as a kind of launch pad for the descending line.

Bar two features a descending sequence with the E Minor Pentatonic scale organized in 4th intervals. In bar three, after playing some lower register notes, we launch into a final blues phrase in bar four.

Example 6k

Here is another E Minor Pentatonic sequence, with the notes organized into quintuplets. You know the drill by now… go slow with a metronome to begin with and gradually speed up!

Example 6l

Here's a simpler E Minor Pentatonic scale sequence to try. Check your fingering here and make sure you're executing this in the most efficient way to achieve a smooth sound.

Example 6m

Here's another challenge for you: an E Minor Pentatonic sequence with some eleven-note groupings!

I don't want you to think that I'm counting something like this in my head, because in truth a fast line like this is a matter of feel, and that is difficult to convey in notation without it looking pretty scary.

To tackle this idea, first of all get the shape of the notes under your fingers. Just play the patterns with no regard for timing and train your fingers to go where you need them to.

Then listen carefully to the audio several times and get the phrasing in your ears. (If it seems too fast, you can use an app such as the Amazing Slow Downer to slow it down without changing the pitch).

Now work on one bar at a time until you begin to get the timing. When you're able to nail each section of the idea separately, work on bringing it all together.

Example 6n

Here is another free-flowing idea that floats over the groove as the tune transitions from one section into the next. An E Blues scale lick opens this idea, while the rest of the line can be seen as E Minor Pentatonic augmented by the two notes from the E Natural Minor scale. The notation documents what was played, but you need to listen closely to the audio to capture the feel and timing.

Example 6o

Next, here is an E Minor Pentatonic line with a borrowed Bb note from the E Blues scale. Here, the opening 1/4 note triplets, then the dotted 1/8th notes throughout, work together to create the effect of making this line sit behind the beat, pulling back at the groove. It's meant to be played with a lazy, laidback feel.

Example 6p

To close out the solo, here is one more E Minor Pentatonic line with a borrowed blue note. It's a busy line and the idea behind it was to begin by playing counterpoint ideas to the low keyboard part, but gradually come into line with it, so that the bass and keys are playing the same rhythm but different notes by the end.

The main thing to look out for here is timing. Listen to the audio and take account of the rests that break up the line.

Example 6q

Conclusion

I hope you've found this deep dive into soloing with the pentatonic scale a useful and informative journey. My aim has been to build on the pentatonic system that we know so well, and show you different ways of augmenting and enhancing it.

The end goal of musical endeavor is always to increase our musical vocabulary, because the wider our vocabulary is, the more we'll be able to express ourselves and have something interesting to say in every musical situation.

Moving forward, I recommend spending time with the following ideas:

1. Work on scale sequencing ideas. We know that the pentatonic scale has a fairly predictable sound, but well-conceived scale sequences can "disguise" it and make it sound more interesting. We looked at several approaches for doing this, but there are many more to discover! For example, try experimenting with playing the scale in diatonic 4ths or 5ths, and move through every position of the scale across the neck. If you get stuck, look into the pentatonic patterns of saxophonist Jerry Bergonzi, who has published some great material.

2. Practice augmenting the pentatonic shapes. To practice adding additional notes into the pentatonic framework, I suggest beginning with just one note. It could be the b5 of the blues scale, for example. Work with this note and add it into all your pentatonic shapes. Drill it right across the fretboard until you can visualize exactly where that note is in every shape. Then put on a backing track and jam with it. Introducing one tension note at a time and working with it thoroughly is much better than being baffled by a huge array of options. Just develop these ideas slowly.

3. Apply rhythmic variation. When you're confident with the shape of an enhanced pentatonic pattern you've been working with, begin to apply different rhythms. Use a metronome and work with it in 1/8th notes, then 1/8th note triplets, then 1/16th notes, then perhaps quintuplets. Next, jam over a backing track and mix and match these rhythms.

4. Build motif-like phrases. Having done all of the above work to master an aspect of the scale, bring everything back to focus on playing strong, melodic, vocal-like phrases. Take your time when building a solo and make sure you have a good mix of vocal phrases that use long notes and articulation, as well as faster, rhythmically complex sequences.

5. Listen. Finally, above all, listen widely and take something from every musician or piece of music that inspires you. Don't just listen to bass players – we can learn from any soloist.

I wish you all the best on your musical journey.

Jimmy.

About the Author

Jimmy was born in the Bronx, New York, and grew up in Huntingdon, Long Island. Aged 13, he became interested in electric bass and has been playing ever since. He moved to Los Angeles in the mid-70s, where he began touring and recording with many different popular artists.

In 1978, he met Robben Ford and keyboardist Russell Ferrante and formed a group to record Robben's first solo recording on Electra-Asylum. The critically acclaimed *The Inside Story* became a landmark recording, which led to the formation of The Yellowjackets, and in 1980 they recorded their debut album for Warner Bros. Records.

In addition to a long tenure with The Yellowjackets, Jimmy has worked across the musical spectrum with such artists as Jeff Lorber, Eric Marienthal, Bruce Hornsby, Rita Coolidge, Gino Vannelli, Kiss, Tommy Bolin, Allan Holdsworth, Marylin Scott, Chaka Khan, Al Jarreau, Donald Fagen and Anita Baker.

Jimmy has won three Grammys for his work, and been nominated a further seventeen times. He has recently been touring and recording with Oz Noy and Jeff Lorber, and arranges and produces projects for many other artists.

www.ingramcontent.com/pod-product-compliance
Lightning Source LLC
Chambersburg PA
CBHW081437090426

42740CB00017B/3340